Aphorisms - Aphrodisms

Hiltrud Schinzel

Aphorisms - Aphrodisms

Aphorisms

Bibliografische Information der Deutschen
Nationalbibliothek:
Die Deutsche Nationalbibliothek verzeichnet diese
Publikation in der Deutschen Nationalbibliografie;
detaillierte bibliografische Daten sind im Internet über
http://dnb.dnb.de abrufbar.

Cover: Ink drawings by the author
Translated from German by Ryan Eyers & Sam Langer for
Gegensatz Translation Collective.

Herstellung und Verlag: BoD – Books on Demand,
Norderstedt

ISBN: 9783756232116

Aphorisms – Aphrodisms

A:

Time is the **a**bstraction of life

Every **a**bstraction is also a reduction

Human **a**ction is largely reactionary

It is not reason but rather prejudice that determines **a**ction in a crisis

Administration is always hobbling at least a half-century behind the times

The inflation of the **a**dministrative apparatus by means of computer technology renders it immobile

Aesthetics is no devotee of theory

Aesthetics can sometimes be sacrificed in service of pedagogy

When it comes to affection, men are like black holes—they suck it all up and offer none in return

Why be afraid of black holes? They might be the most amazing thing you can experience

In adolescence, it is what we want to be that counts; in old age, what we haven't been

With age, modesty becomes pointless, if not life-threatening

With age, hope is replaced by oblivion

Old age: your memory goes while your belly grows

From a certain age, you get a bulk discount on letters of condolence

The aged babble like infants, and the young don't have much to say either

If you are able to see illness as a form of entertainment, ageing can be amusing

Ageing is when everything that previously only caused discomfort becomes life-threatening

Aggressors like to disguise themselves as the besieged

Alcohol consumption is a gauge of your mental state

The **al**coholic drinks his loved ones to death

Alcohol is a jealous lover that permits no other relationships

Nothing makes you feel more **a**live than being **s**ick

Ambition and hysteria march in lockstep

Angst about ageing is best left to the young

The flaneur is like an **a**nt without an anthill
The tourist is like an **a**nt walking around with its entire colony

Anthropocentrists think of nature as a kind of happy, uneducated idiot, because they are incapable of perceiving let alone recognizing any other structure than their own

Remember that wonderful time before the invention of probability theory—when **a**nything was possible?

Not all **a**phorisms lend themselves to the cultural coddling that is wellness

Archives are where knowledge goes to die

A healthy amount of ignorance won't protect you from **a**rrogance

ART:

The architect protects us from the world; the artist creates art in order to understand it; the writer interprets it; the dancer prances upon it; the musician reconciles us with it in waves of sound. None of these can succeed without the other, and we cannot survive without all of them.

The sensory organs assemble the ingredients and somewhere there is a kind of chef who mixes everything together. This is then served in the stock pot that is the artwork; anyone can eat it, but the soup is not to everyone's taste.

The mind is slower than the eye. We design in order to comprehend. It takes much longer to comprehend something than it does to design it.

Why this frantic, incessant drive to combine the old with the new? The old is old and the new is new. They both amount to the same thing. Mixing the two, however, is often a sign of bad taste.

The eye has no need for words

Futurism: The analysis and academicization of art go hand in hand with its infantilization.

Gallerists are people who go around offering (financial) value judgements of art without being asked

History paintings are unbearable en masse but preferred by the public

Iconography is like a dress: it more or less (as the case may be) intentionally obscures intentions.

When it comes to creativity, it is only freedom and not deadlines that will inspire great work

Art has always failed to live up to its ideals: striving too hard for material refinement has resulted in material collapse. Ideals that have strayed too far from their realizability have found their limits in mathematical symbols (Malevich's dots and quadrants etc.) and speculations. Overly ambitious aspirations for social reform have ended in revolution and/or banality.

Art makes you alone without making you lonely

Art is the emotions' way of eluding science's burden of proof

Art supplants the principle of "understanding qua knowledge" with "understanding via experience"

Art should not be treated like Nibelungen treasure: it is not to be hoarded.

The Dusseldorf School and the Nazarenes: the heart opens and the mind shuts.

On the media: you naturally understand more of the world when you grasp its spatiality

Modernity: the artefacts of modernity are the ruins of broken dreams

Postmodern art is characterized by an endless pursuit of the new (e.g., new media, new groups of the marginalized, new possibilities within advertising, etc.) In this way it is always behind the times. Because technological developments are so fast, art will never catch up; thus, the visions and the innovations are now to be found in the realm of technology, and not postmodern art. Instead, this art reflects the everyday chaos that this technology leaves in its wake, as well as the egomania of modern-day human beings and their lack of discernment. Art's irony is the result of a fear of being forced to offer a definitive opinion. As a result, it is materially as well as ideologically just as chaotic as our modern-day environment.

Pre-modern art provides answers, post-modern art asks questions

Art restorers are the defenders in the doomed war against time

Signatures are only good for dating things

Since there are no longer any objectifiable criteria for the evaluation of art, prices are no longer determined by quality but rather the stupidity of its potential new owners

Surrealism is modernity's escape key

Symmetry is utopia

Any song can be turned into a Wagner opera, but is that really necessary?

When all of the AAA art has disappeared into the boardrooms and other vaults of banks, insurance companies, and the like, will we then, as mere minions of the wealthy, have to make do with photographic portraits of these property-hoarding alpha animals exhibited in public, and align our taste to their absurd physiognomies, just as the Roman plebeians of late antiquity did to the hypnotic manga eyes of the Caesars?

Art critics and castrati: they may sing, perhaps even well, but are impotent

Modern-day art history: you either praise a work uncritically or spout faux-intellectual nonsense about it

Commercial art is characterized by its unique ability to bore

The "art market" has nothing to do with art, or with the market as a method for trade – but it does have to do with fraud

In times of upheaval, art is dominated by narrative. Abstraction requires a closed worldview.

Art reveals our woundedness and in the process heals it

Art is humanity's conscience—sometimes good, sometimes bad

Art is Münchhausen's pigtail for everyone

Artistic freedom means contemplating the visible, audible, tangible, and smellable by making things visible, audible, tangible, and smellable.

The artists of the 17th century knew that you can only capture the sky if you have both of your feet firmly on the ground

Artists are people who are incapable of enduring a full day at the office

Artists: they have nothing, but what they don't have they happily give away.

Only the artist is permitted to saw away at the tree of knowledge

The romantic artist is too honest to be truthful

The artwork represents the artist's truth as well as the observer's. It may not be the same truth, but also contains no lies

*The less an **a**rtwork directly offers up, the more nonsense you can attribute to it*

Those who whinge and moan get more out of life: more **a**ttention, at least, if not more recognition

There is nothing more traditional than an erstwhile **a**vant-garde

Reason doesn't stand a chance against **a**varice

Too little **a**wareness is stupid, too much makes you sick

For those who lack **a**wareness, only numbers remain

Awareness lies hidden between the vista and the close-up

B

Abundance structures thinking just as much as lack. Striking an individual **b**alance between them isn't everyone's thing.

Banality is a foreign concept to nature—just like a straight line

Viruses don't have **b**ank accounts

Can **b**anks defeat tanks?

Beauty transcends the dialectic of truth

Beauty that is no longer prized for its own sake but is only valued for the status it affords ceases to have any true value at all

What would be the point of **b**eauty without finality?

Beethoven's 9th Symphony: once again he curses his way through joy

"Nothing nothings" (Heidegger). Perhaps—but **b**eing *is*

The more complexes people have, the more they think they know **b**etter

Don't strive for what is **b**etter before you can discern what is good

One suspects that the **Big B**ang that is supposed to have kickstarted the universe was the sound of a frustrated mother goddess breaking wind and inviting Mother Nature to take part in a duet

Blood is thicker than water but definitely thinner than money

In the human **b**ody, it is the gut that understands first, then the brain, and finally the heart

Neoliberal **b**ook-keeping: that which has been obtained by fraud must be re-invested in bribery

If generating fake news becomes a long-term habit, the **b**rain may conceivably lose the ability to grasp the impact of truth

c

The **c**alf is only respected if it is golden

Within a short space of time, **c**apitalism has turned all our minds to mush

Capitalism is the best form of communism because it turns the masses into customers and the customer is king

No scientific description can be as precise as a **c**aricature

Modern-day **C**assandras are like the tabloid press: they sensationalize that which they have never experienced themselves

Chance is more reliable than human stupidity, including one's own

It is my firm belief that one starts chattering away in order to avoid thinking

In the past, children respected their parents. Nowadays, parents fear their children.

As documented by Abraham, children are conceived out of narcissism and sacrificed at the altar of self-interest

Civilization is a thin crust, reason a rarity, and life a dance atop a volcano

Classiness is a fine thing—but isn't measured in cigarettes

People are only clever when they have to be

Cleverness and cunning are mutually exclusive

Everyone only has a limited amount of compassion, and they need it for themselves

Computers cause decision-making difficulty

The more that logic is handed over to computers, the more the world will descend into chaos

Consumers and narcissists alike make everything about themselves

The best conversationalists are also the best listeners

It is common practice in every discipline to refer to stealing as "cooperation"

Coronavirus: a school of autonomy that does not consist in demonstrating

Corrupt nations have corrupt citizens because corrupt citizens elect corrupt politicians

Dependencies resulting from corruption are inescapable prisons

Corruption is a debt that can never be repaid

If you do not have the courage to stand up for what you believe in, then everything you say will lack meaning

Small countries are often small-minded

Creativity is often linked to illness because just like an illness, a creative phase often announces itself in the form of a bad mood

Crises bring out the greedy pig in us all

The fact that banking **c**rises get managed, but the climate crisis doesn't proves that keeping up appearances is more important than solving problems

A **c**ritic is a fat caterpillar that lives on a steady diet of butterflies

Many people adopt a skewed perspective on reality in order to continue being able to enjoy **c**riticizing (it)

Critique is meaningless as long as it is being funded by those being critiqued

Cowardice is often camouflaged with aggression

D

If 3**D** production is possible, it should also be possible to invent De-Production by similar means

You can't call the **d**ead to the checkout

The **d**ead are rarely interested in eulogies

Death only becomes an important topic to people with too much time on their hands

Death is not an unsympathetic figure: even though it is never loved, it is our most honest and incorruptible friend

Being disconnected from reality means that you consider the journalistic documentation of **d**eath to be an action film or extreme advertising

Some people don't realize that **d**eath means more than just inheritance until it is their turn

Death and the afterlife will likely be just as you imagine—and if not, then at least you'll be surprised

Ever since the world has been governed by **d**eception, everyone has become fond of moralizing—it's sickening

Demo: It's a fine line between community spirit and mass hysteria.

The nice thing about **d**emocracy is that when you have nothing to lose you can still afford to have an opinion

Denial is demented

The more vehemently something is **d**enied, the larger the feeling of guilt

Dictatorships can be deadly, while democracies are merely mind-numbing

It is better to leave something **d**ifficult unfinished than to finish doing something stupid

Discipline without heart leads to much suffering and stomach pain

Documentation: Nothing is lost—except for discernment

The scientific curiosity of the **d**og far surpasses that of the human

E

When it comes to **e**ducating children, people hope to avoid old mistakes while failing to notice new ones

The problem with **e**ducators is that they want to change others and not themselves

That which calls itself **e**lite is usually only mediocre, if not worse

True **e**lites don't need to praise themselves

Perhaps **e**motionality is merely a lack of composure

Even though the opposite is always claimed to be true: you must never expect the same **e**mpathy from your partner or your family than that which your friends can and want to give

Life under the bell jar of steady **e**mployment is safe, but also boring

There is a fine line between **e**nlightening someone and insulting them

The best kind of **e**ntertainment is forgetting about yourself

Everything that becomes playful is comforting, everything that is supposed to work must carelessly injure. **E**thical action is unattainable.

Ethics are only invoked when they are lacking

Euthanasia is the belief that one can only face the fear of death by means of suicide

Evil lacks the power of persuasion: no-one knows what it is good for

Evil is so stupid that we must free it from itself out of pity

Excess ends in exitus

The **e**xcess makes excess work

The best way to **e**xit this world is to drift softly off to sleep...

Consciously or otherwise, everyone constructs their worldview out of **e**xperience

A lot of people today are selling common sense as expert knowledge

The eye sees things differently than the tape measure or the camera

F

Facts are facts and schnapps are schnapps. Facts + schnapps = ERR

Failure is the essence of the future

Faith is a way of making sense of what you don't understand

Stinginess is readily re-packaged as "family interests"

Fantasy can create a universe from a speck of dust

Communities of fate tend to produce the desire for revenge rather than solidarity

The brutality of fear is very democratic: it knows no borders

War isn't the father of all things; fear is the mother of war and thus of all war-fathers

Men's fears drive women to emancipation

The eternal **fe**minine draws us along—and now stupid sayings get the job done. Why? This means (as it always has): now we're really in a mess—sort it out, girlie, and pronto!

As long as Wagner remains a celebrated **f**igure, peace should not be expected

People who have never experienced **f**inancial difficulty fail to grasp that survival is more important than leaving an inheritance

In order to really like someone, you must recognize their **f**laws

A **f**lurry of activity can as easily camouflage stupidity as ill will

People act the **f**ool because they think that others are still more foolish

In every field, many terms which sound professional were invented to mask **f**raudulence

If everyone is cheating, then everything is permitted—except **f**reedom

Freedom is the preserve of the unenvious

Personal **f**reedom can be found in the bathroom mirror each morning

Freedom has many faces

Freedom in a pandemic means being able to die due to your own stupidity rather than that of others

Freedom means asking others for their opinion in order to be able to communicate with them

It is harder to get rid of enemies than friends

The most enduring friendships have a shared skeleton in the closet

If you glorify futility, you're bound to be disappointed

Some people are not afraid of the future because they don't know what it is

G

The human gaze is a one-way street—it only can only go in a single direction

True geniuses know how stupid they are

Our goals often blind us

I do not believe in God, but I have nothing against him existing

Happy is the one who seeks to do **g**ood, while those who want what is good all for themselves are doomed to unhappiness

You don't know what you've **g**ot (and how much it's worth!) 'til it's gone

If you yourself are **g**reat, then it's easy to let others be as great as they are
If you yourself are small, then you have to make others smaller than you
If you isolate yourself, then you'll be neither here nor there, for you lack comparison

Money is not obtained through performance but rather by **g**reed

Greed is self-destructive

Whatever type or breed, all beings die from **g**reed.

Nothing is as serious as **g**reed would have you believe

Greed and nationalism are identical twins

The only true communist is the **G**rim Reaper

If absolutely everything must be forced to **g**row, then let it finally be in the right direction!

One can only live with **g**uilt when one accepts fault—
including that of one's parents

H

Hate is infatuation turned on its head

If you want to play God, it helps to have the **h**eavens
on your side

Every system creates hypocrites and **h**eroes,
sometimes within the same person

According to Frans de Waal, only in humans does
hierarchy lead to megalomania. But it can also produce
elegant results, —take the Eiffel Tower, for example.

Homo sapiens: a peacock that still cannot correctly
count its feathers!

Hope is a beautiful thing, as long as it doesn't collapse
into expectation

It can be so restorative to give up **h**ope—you see
things much more clearly and can judge proportionally
again

Human action is largely reactionary

The **h**uman primate loves to mark its territory with
waste, war waste in particular

Humanity sits perched atop a pile of trash that it maintains is a treasure trove!

Humans consist of things remembered and things forgotten, between which a briefly illuminated moment of experience is embedded

When humans invented the straight line, they sacrificed beauty for the benefit of utility

Humans are the only living creatures that allow themselves to be oppressed by their own inventions

Humour is the only escape from brutality and chaos

Difficult times require a sense of humour. Only in good times can seriousness be tolerated

Humour is a form of self-defence that you can teach yourself

Hysteria transforms memory into a photo negative

Some people become hysterical as soon they have to do without that which others have never had

Hysterics can still spoil the last days of life for themselves and others

I

The ideal always jars with its realization, and thus its achievability must often be constantly deferred to the afterlife

Some have to bear children others ideas

Some fall ill from overwork, while others fall prey to idleness

Beyond love and hate lies indifference

Homo sapiens girds itself against information overload by retreating into code and the binary system

Whenever someone tells you that "it's in your best interest", you can be sure that it is in theirs

Investment banks and politics: rewarding thieves with money will not turn them honest

J

Jeans have replaced grey trousers as the uniform of private life

Journalism's charm lies in the fact that every piece of news contains at least one mistake

People prefer presents to justice

K

Sooner or later, every **K**ing Kong turns out to be a pipsqueak

Know-it-alls know loneliness on their deathbeds

Knowledge is often mistaken for arrogance

Democracy painstakingly worms its way through the gap that exists between arrogance and **k**nowledge

My **k**nowledge is the sum total of my failures

The more **k**nowledge you have, the more mistakes you make

Too much **k**nowledge deadens the mind

Knowledge is power. Knowing better is a struggle for power.

Knowledge is power. Arrogance is powerlessness.

The more someone **k**nows, the more they make the simplest things complicated

L

It's good to learn to be able to **l**augh at yourself, because there's no finer sound than laughter

So much has become **l**aughable that there is nothing left to laugh about

People talk so much nonsense that language should be banned

Laws become necessary when common sense takes its leave

We suffer from their effects, but we also need the security that lies provide

No-one can claim to be the first to have become trapped in their own web of lies

Unfortunately, life is not a mathematical problem that can be solved by a statistic plucked from thin air

Learn to endure life without making it unbearable for others

Even though anyone can give their own life meaning, no-one has yet figured out the meaning of life

What is the point of life? To live or to be distracted from life?

It's easy to drive a hard bargain when you only have your own life to lose

A difficult life is a quick pathway to becoming smart; a hedonist, in contrast, has no chance

Acting rationally has nothing to do with intelligence and everything to do with life experience

The "good life" makes people do bad things

Life is a journey without travel insurance

Life is a jigsaw puzzle that can only be completed by death

You can only admire who/what you don't have to live with

Lobbyists love to point fingers at anyone but themselves

A person is only lonely if they cannot entertain themselves. This is almost always the case, however. Unfortunately, one must often accept that while one's own company might not be entertaining, it is always the best.

The Lord's Prayer: and deliver us from our desires that refuse to die

The most common form of love is one of convenience

Vices bring people together more than love

What passes for love nowadays seems like a kind of wellness exercise

Love may be blind, but greed is even blinder

He loves me not: he lies only to and not for me!

Effective lying requires a good memory

Lying is uneconomical because it costs you a lot of time

M

The only difference between the mafia and modern-day politicians seems to be that the mafia avoid media coverage

Acting out of malice always appears more logical than acting out of good will

In cultures no longer dependent on hunting mammoths men have become inferior to women

Any relationship with a man, even a purely platonic one, requires a lot of babysitting

Marathon: how can one be so stupid to take pleasure in running when we all know death will catch up with us all in the end?

In the global market economy, nationalistic regimes tend to destroy themselves sooner or later—albeit with enormous collateral damage

In the past, one conquered hearts, countries, and continents; nowadays, one conquers **M**arkets, somewhat of a backward step

For the **m**aterialist, a wife and child means property, decorum, and nursing staff in old age

Apparently you only need a little fame to quickly be deified or demonized in the **m**edia

In our **m**edia-oriented society, even live images of bombings appear to be staged

Collective **m**emory is an unsolvable puzzle made up of individual perceptions

Memory is so manipulative that it often collates facts into watertight lies

Collective **m**emory is an unsolvable puzzle made up of individual perceptions

Men who have nothing to do always think their job is to keep their wives busy

Men who overestimate themselves tend to underestimate their wives

Men want leitmotifs,
women and children want love

The military functions well as long as it sticks to hunting for easter eggs

Our minds are too slow for the speedy tools they have created

Misanthropy can become one of life's highest pleasures

Misery brings people closer than happiness

If you can't admit to a mistake, you will never be rid of it

Every generation has the right to make its own mistakes

You can fix your own mistakes but not (those of) other people

Modesty is always a standard only others should live up to

Why worship money when flowers are more beautiful?

Those who worship money are happy when others worship deities

Money helps you live but also makes you blind

Nowadays everyone bows in the presence of **m**oney, especially when it is stolen

Do not trust those who speak about **m**oney in times of crisis. They will no longer acknowledge you when you don't have any left!

Any domain occupied by **m**oralists is suspect

In **m**otion, everything falls into place; at rest, you fall to pieces

Mountains cast shadows—the taller the mountain, the longer the shadow

Most **m**yths are simply cock-and-bull stories, unfortunately often brilliantly packaged, because your geniuses like Shakespeare adapt them just as often as your Wagners

N

The **n**arcissist demands too much of others and too little of themselves

It may be called **n**avel-gazing, but he who only gazes at his own dick isn't going to find out much about life either. This doesn't apply to the earthworm.

People talk so much **n**onsense that the truth has become lost in the noise

A thought has already become **n**onsense before it has even passed through one's mind, let alone one's lips

Only "**n**ormal" people readily accept the world's madness

Some make a lot out of **n**othing, while others turn a lot into nothing

Ever since the introduction of **n**umbers, we have condemned ourselves to counting

Seeing only in **n**umbers is worse than seeing with your eyes

O

Ever since we've gotten **o**ld, the youth don't know anything anymore

Optimization does not make you a better person

We do not see **o**thers as they are. We only see what our own blinkers of envy and superior posturing want to make of them

P

The **p**andemic is a caricature of the extent to which unnecessary things get in the way of necessary action in human behaviour. One could say that we are still following in the footsteps of the late-Roman model.

A defect uncovered by the **p**andemic: a typical human behaviour seems to be to do exactly the opposite of what is needed.

Panic without consequences is completely pointless

Paradise is where you feel at home—it is to be found within. But only when you are comfortable in your own skin can you be your own paradise.

If you can accept that **p**arents are people with flaws, you have not only grown up, but can then also accept that the world is full of flaws too

Those who criticize the **p**ast readily forget that it cannot meet the needs of the present

You can only see in the **p**ast what you can feel in the present

The **p**ast is like plastic: you cannot get rid of it, but its quality and appearance change

It is more difficult to be **p**atient with oneself than with anybody else

Pathos is never elegant

The **p**athway to the ideal eschews the contours of feeling

Some **p**eople don't know what they are doing, others don't know what they should be doing

It is always the least stable **p**eople who feel most compelled to give advice

Most **p**eople are neither good nor bad. They only want to seem good in front of others while simultaneously feeding their own egos. This leads to dilemmas.

It must be a kind of love-hate relationship with art that drives unartistic **p**eople to study the arts

You will never really get to know a **p**erson as long as you continue to project your own flaws and virtues onto them

Pessimism is a dead end

You can do as you **p**lease as long as you are still able to be pleased with what you can do

Not every banality has to be transformed into a **p**hilosophy

The *ought* of **p**hilosophy must not crush the *is* (of our lives)

Philosophers are the archaeologists of their own present moment: they try to interpret incomprehensible givens/facts.

Some **p**hilosophers think they are prophets when in fact they are only pessimists

The problem with **p**hilosophy is that it forgets that people are living and acting beings

A **p**icture makes the three-dimensional world liveable

Plagiarists can always immediately spot the genuine article

You're not going to turn anyone on by quoting **P**lato, but Kant isn't exactly sexy either

A common tactical error made by **p**oliticians: no pig should forbid another for grunting.

A **p**olitics dependent on voter hysteria is dangerous, but a politics that causes politicians to become hysterical is deadly

A **p**osition is not won as a result of performance or sovereignty but rather as a result of a desire for money and power

When men form a posse, it always ends up as a gang; when women band together, they always end up cooking dinner

What is possible should not become what is required necessary

Postmodernism has snapped us out of our obsession with being objective. Unfortunately, this has been replaced with an obsession with creating systems.

Power is not acquired by being superior but rather by having an insatiable desire for it

Powermongers' insistence on performing their power only points to their preposterousness

The only thing you can expect to understand in the course of your life is your own prejudice

The press lives on the need for attention and thus falls prey to its demands

An object's price does not reflect its quality but rather the stupidity of the people who wish to acquire it

The principle of Cassandrian foresight only works for the stock market and not in reality. People don't react in the way that vested interests and rigid formulae would have you believe. One must therefore leave ego at the door when making preventative decisions.

When it comes down to it, all so-called **p**rivileges ultimately stem from a lineage of theft and fraud

The passing of time will transform even the most outrageous of **p**rovocations into pathetic-seeming trivialities

Q

Quantity trumps not only quality but also rationality

People who always have an answer ready are usually too dumb to ask the right **q**uestions

R

It doesn't take much for a **r**ant to become a whinge

Most people go on **r**ants because the others are stupid enough to listen

The exception is **r**ational, not the rule

Being considerate is more important than being **r**ational

Reality can never catch up to anticipation

If some men devoted as much care to their partners as they did to gnawing a chicken drumstick, many **r**elationships would have a good chance of success

Religion is about continually offering consolation in the afterlife, as if this life weren't trouble enough

Religion is often much more empathetic than science

Religions don't make people better, but they do help them feel better

The only thing you can really rely on is your own wickedness

Only the replica offers the possibility of the infinite

If you want to scare a man off, ask him to take responsibility for something

If you want to get rich, having a bad character will suffice—intelligence tends to get in the way

The rich think themselves to be altruists when receiving gifts from the poor

The purpose of ridicule is always to divert attention from one's own flaws

Routine gobbles up enjoyment

A rule is pointless if not pursued

S

Saving is an offshoot of squandering

Between **s**aying and being lies the entire world

Science: the more work you put into an experiment, the less valuable the results.

Science creates visuals without having learnt the rules of art and aesthetics

Science purports to be agnostic but strongly believes in statistics

There are areas of life in which **s**cience has nothing to uncover

Science without empathy is shameless

Ever since the **s**ciences took charge, we have been constantly subjected to a stupefying barrage of euphoria surrounding the supposed supremacy of "verifiability"

Only what is **s**cientifically correct can be successfully manipulated

The **s**cientist is always teetering between having an inferiority complex and delusions of grandeur

Scientists are never as clever as what they say

Security gained at another's expense will not keep you safe for long

Self-sacrifice in service of an ideal only works in (religious) theory, not in practice

The senior clutches at his chest, not ready to be laid to rest!

The senior should eat from his plate, and not forget to chew at that!

Common sense means striking a balance between prejudice and knowing better

Only the sensitive soul can be or become strong

We all carry the baggage of our supposed seriousness

Sexiness and matronliness are two rungs on the same ladder

The best way to punish a sinner is to pardon them

Whether ski lift or Sisyphus, both are beholden to gravity

Social security rots your brain

Despite this, it is obviously difficult to make a society centred around hedonism suddenly prioritize sacrifice without dangling a carrot

In a society whose currency is bullshit, one's opinions must be instantaneous—thinking is taboo.

Sociology: truisms repackaged in sophisticated language

If you can't do something you have to get someone else to do it for you

Crossing something out is more fun than writing it down

Just because the soul resides in nerve cells does not necessarily mean it is a materialist

It's fun to speculate, even if you end up being wrong

Stinginess is readily re-packaged as "family interests"

Stupid gossip is like saying rosaries: nonsense finds its way into your brain through repetition

It takes a lot of talk to mask stupidity, while wisdom often only requires a few words

Stupidity is a contagious disease, intelligence isn't

Stupidity ends in death—unfortunately it's usually someone else's

Stupidity always prevails because it does not experience doubt

It makes more sense to want to save the world from one's own stupidity than from that of others

Stupidity is dumb but seldom mute

The stupidity of structures affects their users as a factor with exponential growth potential

If you take every instance of stupidity seriously, you'll stymie your ability to overcome them

There is a decent portion of stupidity in unscrupulousness

The only people who extol the virtue of suffering are those who have not experienced it

The less someone suffers, the more they complain

Superiority works by denying the other person what is important to them

Every kind of systemic language, such as mathematics, paradoxically destroys that which is self-evident

T

Ever since death has become a taboo, crime novels have exploded in popularity

The majority of people become teachers because they don't know what else to do

One is only able to shed tears when the cruelty that provoked them becomes bearable

The only "democratic" technology is Sisyphus' rolling stone

Technology has become so complex that it has become its own obstacle

Modern technology has caused the world to become swamped with dilettantes

Our gums are only too happy to bid rotten teeth farewell

People with straight teeth usually have a crooked mouth

Why does theory always insist on trying to be smarter than practice?

Reading too much theory causes you to lose your instinct, if not your mind

Some thieves have had to learn to thank their victims—the beneficiaries of colonial theft, for example. A small piece of political progress that is yet to translate to private life.

Deadlines are not created because of a lack of time but rather a desire to extort

Time has many facial features, including the patient gaze of Penelope and the searching eye of Odysseus

Christmas trees on the sidewalk: times are such that it won't be long until we'll be grateful to be able to make soup out of pine needles!

These days, the pathway to the gallows and to the toilet are both taken on foot. Louis the XIV didn't need to take either, which some regret.

Tourism causes travellers to recede to the developmental level of hunter-gatherers

In Austria, the present twinkles with sugar-coated Hapsburgian history for tourists

You can't get through life without a bit of trust, although it is difficult to survive being betrayed

The truth is usually insulting

Yesterday's truth rarely ends up being today's

People love to bury the truth beneath thousands of irrelevant details

Every truth has an expiry date

Truth is the lie you like to believe best

Nothing is as annoying as a truth borne out by facts

U

We most readily despise what we do not **u**nderstand

Utopias are laudable but often adolescent and occasionally even dangerous

v

If everything becomes **v**irtual, there will be nothing left to eat

The more a person brags about their apparent **v**irtue, the more debauchery they are trying to hide

The **v**oice of reason is oft derided

Many people take a **v**oyeuristic view of their fellows, seeing their misery as a form of entertainment

W

It's nicer to **w**anna, but sometimes you've just gotta

When you don't get what you **w**ant, pretend that you want what you already have instead—it's much easier that way

The cheers of football fans can quickly descend into cries of **w**ar

When it comes to **w**ar nowadays, what counts isn't how much blood is spilled but rather how much the market moves

Only the **w**eak feel that they must perform strength

One can only tolerate others' **w**eaknesses when they do not try to portray them as strengths

As a rule, the distribution of **w**ealth is based on theft, and inherited stolen goods rarely survive three generations

Uniformity of dress allows camouflaged **w**ealth to infiltrate poverty

The good thing about poverty is that you can better enjoy moments of sporadic prosperity. The bad thing about **w**ealth is that it doesn't know about poverty

Other people's **w**eddings are much more fun than one's own

Nowadays we see everything as through a **w**ide-angle lens—partly out of desire, partly out of greed: a lust for longing.

Once you've started writing your **w**ill, it's much more difficult to stop

Wisdom = the remorse you feel immediately after making a mistake

Although it is unclear whether **w**isdom will survive, it is certain that stupidity will dig its own grave

There is no stupider proverb than "The **w**iser head gives in". The wise head who gives in is in fact the stupid one, which means that it is the stupider head that gives in and not the wise one.

We first get to know our **w**ishes once they have been fulfilled

Many **w**omen prefer to have a breadwinner in their beds than work on their desks

Women can plump their lips, while men often prefer to puff up their chests

You can get away with a lot more nonsense in **w**ord than in deed

If you're going to talk tough, you must be prepared to choke on your **w**ords!

No-one believes a word of what **w**ords have to say any more

Nowadays people would rather **w**ork themselves to death than take some time to think

Work doesn't set you free, doing nothing even less so

The pleasures of the world of **w**ork:
Under communism, you couldn't do anything about bad pay

Under capitalism, you can work yourself to death without pay
Under socialism, a couple of stupid busy bees work themselves into the ground for an excess of clever slackers

Once again, humanity appears to be sleeping through the end of the world

The world has become a classroom in which the self-appointed teachers—the credit rating agencies—give lessons on greed and envy by banning snacks.

The world is not a battleground for ants—even if some ants believe it to be so

For those who don't know anything the world is still full of surprises

We never forgive those whom we wrong

The author thanks Ryan Eyers & Sam Langer and Gegensatz Translation Collective for their sensitive and skillful translation from German.